# First hundred words

Heather Amery

Illustrated by Stephen Cartwright

Language consultant: Betty Root
Edited by Jenny Tyler
Designed by Mike Olley and Jan McCafferty

There is a little yellow duck to find in every picture.

# The living room

Daddy

Mummy

boy

girl baby dog cat

3

# Getting dressed

shoes

pants

jumper

4

vest      trousers      t-shirt      socks

# The kitchen

bread

milk

eggs

6

apple

orange

banana

# Tidying up

table

chair

plate

8

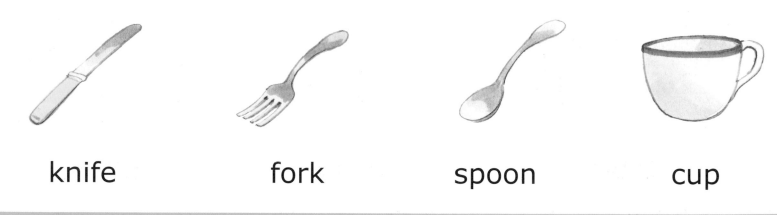

knife     fork     spoon     cup

# Play time

horse          sheep          cow

hen pig train bricks

# Going on a visit

Granny

Grandpa

slippers

12

coat      dress      hat

# The park

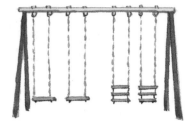

tree          flower          swings          ball

14

slide boots bird boat

# The street

car

bicycle

plane

truck          bus          house

# Having a party

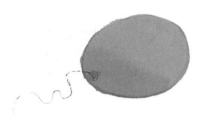
balloon

cake

clock

ice cream　　　fish　　　biscuits　　　sweets

19

# Going swimming

arm

hand

leg

feet          toes          head          bottom

# The changing room

mouth

eyes

ears

22

nose        hair        comb        brush

23

# Going shopping

red

blue

green

yellow　　　　pink　　　　white　　　　black

# Bath time

soap

towel

toilet

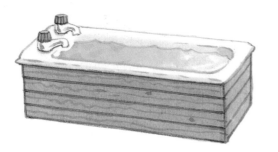 **bath**

 **tummy**

 **duck**

# Bed time

bed

lamp

window

28

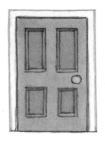   

door book doll teddy

29

# Match the words to the pictures

apple

ball

banana

book

boots

cake

car

cat

clock

cow

dog

doll

duck

egg

fish

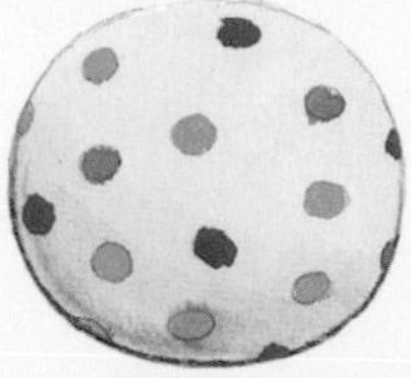

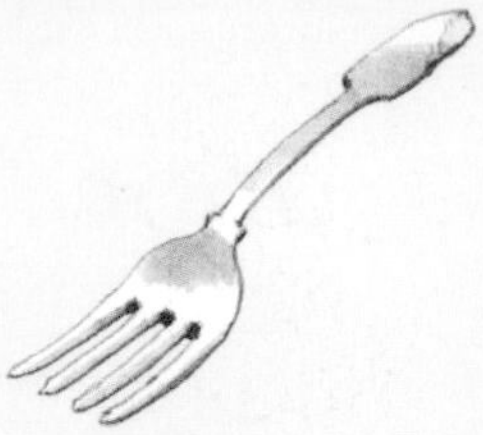

fork

hat

ice cream

jumper

knife

lamp

milk

orange

pig

socks

table

teddy

train

vest

window

# Counting

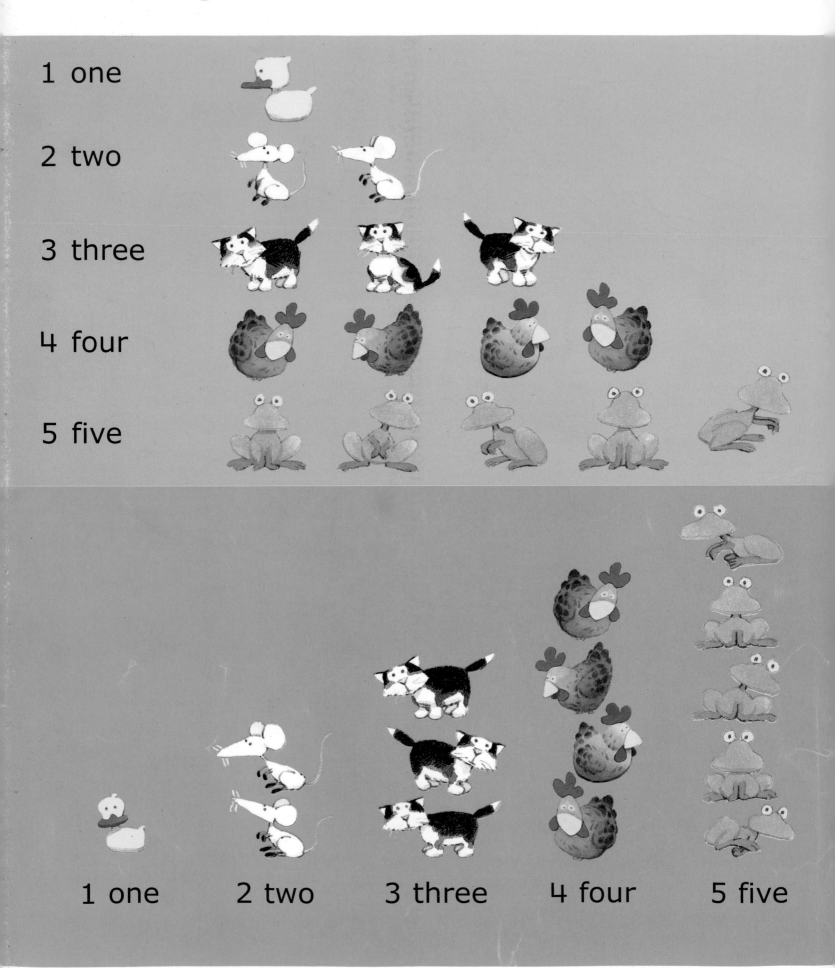

1 one

2 two

3 three

4 four

5 five

1 one     2 two     3 three     4 four     5 five

This edition first published in 2009 by Usborne Publishing Ltd, Usborne House, 83-85 Saffron Hill, London EC1N 8RT, England. www.usborne.com Copyright © 2009, 2001 Usborne Publishing Ltd.
The name Usborne and the devices ♈ ⊕ are Trade Marks of Usborne Publishing Ltd. All rights reserved. No part of this publication may be reproduced, stored in a retrieval system, or transmitted in any form or by any means, electronic, mechanical, photocopying, recording or otherwise without the prior permission of the publisher.
Printed in Shenzhen, Guangdong, China.